Albert Einstein

by Lola M. Schaefer
and Wyatt S. Schaefer

Consulting Editor: Gail Saunders-Smith, Ph.D.
Consultant: Daniel Marlow, Ph.D., Professor and Chair
Physics Department, Princeton University
Princeton, New Jersey

Pebble Books

an imprint of Capstone Press
Mankato, Minnesota

Pebble Books are published by Capstone Press
151 Good Counsel Drive, P.O. Box 669, Mankato, Minnesota 56002
http://www.capstone-press.com

Library of Congress Cataloging-in-Publication Data
Schaefer, Wyatt, 1987–
    Albert Einstein / by Wyatt Schaefer and Lola M. Schaefer.
    p. cm.—(First biographies)
    Includes bibliographical references and index.
    Contents: Early Life—Changes in physics—Famous Albert.
    ISBN 0-7368-2079-5 (hardcover)
    1. Einstein, Albert, 1879–1955—Juvenile literature. 2. Physicists—Biography—
Juvenile literature. [1. Einstein, Albert, 1879–1955. 2. Physicists. 3. Scientists.]
I. Schaefer, Lola M., 1950- II. Title. III. Series: First biographies (Mankato, Minn.)
QC16.E5 S287 2004
530'.092—dc21
                                                                          2002155660

Note to Parents and Teachers

The First Biographies series supports national history standards for units on people and culture. This book describes and illustrates the life of Albert Einstein. The photographs support early readers in understanding the text. This book also introduces early readers to subject-specific vocabulary words, which are defined in the Words to Know section. Early readers may need assistance to read some words and to use the Table of Contents, Words to Know, Read More, Internet Sites, and Index/Word List sections of the book.

Table of Contents

Time Line

1879
born

4

Albert Einstein was born
in Germany in 1879.
Albert was shy.
He did not talk much.

◄ Albert (right) stands with his sister Maria in 1888.

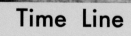

Time Line

1879
born

Albert had many talents.
He played the violin.
He was a good student
in math and science.

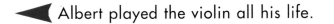
Albert played the violin all his life.

Time Line

1879
born

1896
begins
college

1902
begins working
in patent office

Albert went to college in Switzerland. He studied physics and math. After college, Albert worked in a patent office. A patent office helps inventors.

Time Line

1879	1896	1902	1905
born	begins college	begins working in patent office	writes about the speed of light

In 1905, Albert wrote that nothing could move faster than the speed of light. This idea changed the way people think about movement in the universe.

Time Line

1879
born

1896
begins
college

1902
begins working
in patent office

1905
writes about the
speed of light

In 1916, Albert wrote about gravity. His ideas changed the way scientists understand time, space, and gravity.

1916
writes about gravity,
space, and time

Time Line

1879 born	**1896** begins college	**1902** begins working in patent office	**1905** writes about the speed of light

Many people read what
Albert wrote. He talked
to people about his ideas.
He traveled around Europe
and to the United States.
Albert became famous.

1916
writes about gravity,
space, and time

Time Line

| 1879 born | 1896 begins college | 1902 begins working in patent office | 1905 writes about the speed of light |

Albert also wrote about peace. He spoke out against war. He believed that fighting was not a good way to solve problems.

1916
writes about gravity,
space, and time

Time Line

1879
born

1896
begins
college

1902
begins working
in patent office

1905
writes about the
speed of light

In 1933, Albert moved
to Princeton, New Jersey.
He taught physics. Albert
continued to work on
his science experiments.

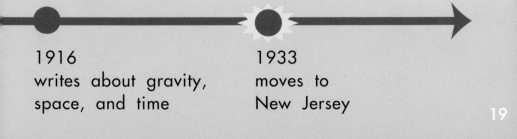

1916
writes about gravity,
space, and time

1933
moves to
New Jersey

Time Line

1879	1896	1902	1905
born	begins college	begins working in patent office	writes about the speed of light

Albert was the most famous scientist of the 1900s. He died in 1955. Albert Einstein's ideas changed the way people understand the universe.

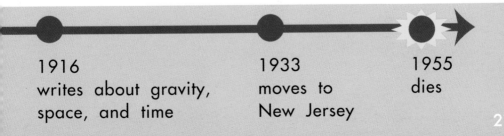

1916
writes about gravity,
space, and time

1933
moves to
New Jersey

1955
dies

Words to Know

college—a school people attend after high school

experiment—a test to learn something new

gravity—a force that pulls objects together; gravity pulls objects toward the center of Earth and keeps them from floating away.

patent—a legal paper that gives an inventor the right to make and sell an item

physics—the science that deals with matter and energy; physics includes the study of light, heat, sound, electricity, motion, and force.

science—the study of nature and the physical world by testing, experimenting, and measuring

scientist—a person who studies science

space—the universe beyond Earth's atmosphere

speed of light—the rate at which light moves; light moves at 186,000 miles (300,000 kilometers) per second.

universe—the planets, the stars, and all items in space

Read More

Rau, Dana Meachen. *Albert Einstein.* Compass Point Early Biographies. Minneapolis: Compass Point Books, 2003.

Reid, Struan. *Albert Einstein.* Groundbreakers. Chicago: Heinemann Library, 2001.

Wyborny, Sheila. *Albert Einstein.* Inventors and Creators. San Diego: Kidhaven Press, 2003.

Internet Sites

Do you want to find out more about Albert Einstein? Let FactHound, our fact-finding hound dog, do the research for you.

Here's how:

1) Visit *http://www.facthound.com*

2) Type in the **Book ID** number: **0736820795**

3) Click on **FETCH IT**.

FactHound will fetch Internet sites picked by our editors just for you!

Index/Word List

Word Count: 189
Early-Intervention Level: 19

Editorial Credits

Martha E. H. Rustad, editor; Heather Kindseth, cover designer and illustrator; Enoch Peterson, production designer; Linda Clavel, illustrator; Kelly Garvin, photo researcher; Karen Risch, product planning editor

Photo Credits

Corbis, 8; Corbis/Bettmann, cover, 1, 18; Lucien Aigner, 16
Getty Images/Hulton Archive, 4, 6, 10, 12, 14, 20